a collection of poetry
by
Nancy Melinda Hunley

Also by Nancy Melinda Hunley:

This Time Around

Cover Design: Melinda Winters
Layout: J. L. Saloff
Fonts: Apple Chancery, Invitation, Porcelain, WebOMints

First Edition

Hunley, Nancy Melinda
   Love in the Middle Ages

ISBN: 0-9742830-1-0
Copyright: TXu1-100-548

"The poems in *Love in the Middle Ages* explore the many emotions of love, from the physical passion of a lover's embrace, to the longing caused by a lover's absence, to the pain of a lover's betrayal. Simple loves of everyday life such as the comfort of flannel sheets on a cold morning and the taste of home-made ice cream are captured. Even the love and companionship of an aging pet is recalled. Can one love too much? If the examples of love in this collection contain the answer, then the answer is no. For to love is to live."

> —Denise Stafford, former columnist for *Senior Living Newspaper* and past board member of the Tennessee Mountain Writers, Inc.

"At the heart of desire you discover an architecture that is attempting to tear itself apart during the very act of creation. These poems chronicle the relationships that develop as a result of this turbulence. Lovers come, go, leave their memory. The dancer refuses to dance alone. The support of others sometimes proves to be a false support. And pulling all these stories together under one roof is the expression of human desire—its longing and rejection, its will and its weaknesses. Here you will see the body praised for its imperfections, and the heart, at its lowest register, as a swamp of "brackish neediness." Yet, these emotions seem temporary—it's obvious that things move on, change, and find different expressions. Listening to all these voices, you begin to realize that it is the searching that matters, that the desire to find out what lies beyond gives these experiences their true value. "Ahead feels/ unfamiliar and raw." And who would have it any other way."

> —Joe Millar, poet.

Table of Contents

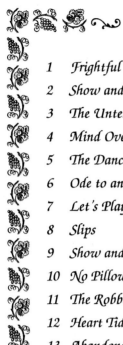

Table of Contents

iv

These poems are dedicated to

—oh, why bother, you know who you are.

Bridges have burned.
Memories, like fires, need tending.
Wandering lost through smoke-filled nights,
I find no haven.
We ventured close at winter's solstice, but
with the approaching equinox,
my want is greater.
I hunger. If only
my heart hadn't played
trumps so soon....
Shedding playground fantasies
first dreamed in girlhood,
I stumble
onward through an unblazed trail
of growth. Ahead feels
unfamiliar and raw.
That I do know
for truth.

I love the feel of a warm southern wind
combing my hair as I walk
by the river on early evenings
when the rich late spring aromas are so arousing
that I'm embarrassed breathing them in.
I love the tangy iciness in my mouth
of homemade peach ice cream on sultry summer afternoons,
chilling my tongue and melting sweetness
slowly down the length of my throat
and cooling the heat in my belly.
I love waking between downy flannel sheets on bright cold fall mornings
while my cats snore softly beside my naked sides,
their furry bodies lending me warmth for the breaking day
and, in that bed, we share assurance of our status
in the greater scheme of the mutual dependency of all life.
I love sitting in my darkened living room
mesmerized by the hot glow of an oak fire,
knowing that there are eight inches of wet heavy snow
blanketing the outdoors beyond my house's sheltering walls,
watching flames reflect their golden dance on the room about me,
with my two companions, their bones melted by the heat,
laid out in long puddles by my feet.
I love finding, during my annual trek up the mountain,
that circle of jacks-in-the-pulpit
standing like a miniature Stonehenge in mottled brown leaf litter,
hidden from all except the most observant eyes.
I love—maybe, I love too freely.

Like downy dandelion tufts
blithely adrift on breezy currents, seeds
holding the promise of love
float lazily by,

tacking
slowly over the fields of our lives.

With sails furled, those
covert passions dock,
perversely putting out roots
where few tender hearts could survive,

ignoring
that a rose out of place is a weed.

And yet, praying that some
among us are better at husbandry
than others, she dreams
that a mountain laurel
will thrive in a citrus grove.

Like Elvis,

you have left the building and, although

you are not here,

I can taste your body on my lips,

I can feel your hands caressing my breasts,

I can sense parts of you inside parts of me

kissing me and stroking me.

My arms are trembly weak

from supporting me above you while

my legs feel as if I have spent

days astride a war horse

battling over hotly contested ground.

With my body aching in places

I didn't even know it had places,

I await your return

for only you

can fill this raw emptiness

I discovered upon your leaving.

> *The spirit is willing*
>
> *even as the body entertains serious doubts*
>
> *about its ability to perform.*

Couples dance as they have for centuries.
Posturing. Posing. It is a pastime in which
I would not willingly choose to participate,
but play at it I must. It is, after all, the only game
in town. Never having been good at imitating
a coy wallflower, I wish the pretenses over and
the music muffled and we were feeling each other's
animal heat, breathing innocently in tandem,
floating in that fuzzy hazy half-world between
dreams and realities where there is no true division
of the two. The male leads, so they say, where
the female directs. It is the thrill of the hunt for him,
the excitement of the chase for her. I want this tarantella
of courtship completed so that we might embark
on the never-ending waltz of our lives moving together. If
you would just quit standing around with your hands in your pockets,
I wouldn't have to dance to the music alone.

Ode to an Old Dog

He howls too loud. His eyesight is going
and his hearing is bad. He snores in his sleep
more often than not. His ears are torn. His body scarred.
His arthritic joints make getting around
on a winter's day an ordeal too painful to watch.
He is an old dog who has run too long in the hunt.
I could clean him up, but I can't take him anywhere.
He crowds his nose in the crotch of every woman he meets,
sugary pretty-pleases whining in his throat, and circles stiff-legged
around every man with taunts rumbling low in his chest.
But I remember him as he was in his prime
and that's how he will live in my mind
long after the old dog is gone.

6

Remember the rooms when we were in grammar school?
Big rectangles of space, greasy-dust smell of oiled wood floors,
and crowded desks so old our parents had carved their initials there.
Across one long wall, double-hung windows stood at attention
and, in the spring, breezes racing in chased papers off our desks.

    Remember?

There were blackboards covering the short wall in front of the room
and along the big wall facing the windows. That longer blackboard
was flanked by two doors with transoms that leaned out
into a cavernous hall. Twin rows of milk glass bowls brimming
with light extended down from the ceiling, each suspended
by a single tarnished brass chain. The supply closet was located
off the short wall in the back. So were coat hooks for us.

    You do remember?

Let's play school. You be the teacher and stand in front
of that old classroom. The blackboards are freshly wiped down in
preparation for today's lesson, giving you that entire space of blank
black slate on which to write. Pick up a fresh length of chalk.
Feel its dry compressed powder between your fingers.
Be prepared to hear its screech as you write. Play pretend
I'm your pupil, hungry to know all you know. Now
teach me what LOVE is. Go ahead. Start. I double-dog dare you.

    Oh, by the way, don't forget, in case we scare ourselves,
    we have separate doors through which to escape.

Occasionally pieces of my past hang out
to haunt me: dingy straps of unhappiness
sneaking off shoulders, tattered dreams
dangling below hem's edge. I prefer to
think I've been happy as the alternative is
an option I care not to explore. I pay scant
attention to my quirky little slips showing,
hoping that no one else will notice
them as well. Choices I made coming up
seemed correct for the time. I opted for
catch-your-breath action. Dull was an
experience to be weeded out. I'm not yet in
my rocking chair at the home and already
have more than a few ricks of memories to
keep me warm come winter. Some say I
could light the match now and have fuel
left over for my pyre. While sane selections
I make today feel drab in comparison, judgments
rule I should have been that way in my youth.
So, who died and made them God? I own
the chaos I created. My little wavelets rippled away,
sometimes tsunamis rumbled back. Still,
some of us never change completely and so,
I continue hoeing my row, parts of those
old slips exposed and all, looking for the next
obstacle in my path, waiting for the uncertainties
of uncultivated choices to quicken my blood.

I have told more than one man I love you,
each instance thinking I spoke truth, but
I have since grown wise
and realize I have
no knowledge of that emotion.
I have wantonly loved too much in my time
and have no utterance to define
what I feel for you,
nor do I know how to show you how I feel
for I have acted out the word so cavalierly over the years
that I don't understand
what it means any more.
Show me
what you know love to be
before we grow too old
and have too little time left to experience
all that we would share
if we loved each other.

Sometimes I think
there is no place where I can mend
my hurting heart. So, hardening myself for a
solitary future, I think me surely safe from harm
until once again, a kindly appearing hand or a
gentle sounding word lures me. And like a scared
hungry abandoned tabby cat, I slink away from my
hidyhole, tempted by that opened outstretched palm and
sweet seductive voice, hoping for one good master,
getting a hard boot to my side instead.
Sometimes I think
there will be no arm on which I can pillow
my weary head. I long for someone to hold me
and shelter me from Life's battering storms. Many
times in the past, I paid for temporary arms with my
body. I will not apologize for that at this late date for it
was the only tender I possessed then, but now I am too old
and too tired to care to barter for a few hours of false warmth.
Sometimes I recall a haunting phrase—it comes
to taunt me now and again . . . Love like
you've never been hurt before. She spoke those words
as she entered a man's strong enclave simply
because he had pledged his protection against approaching
winter's cold and damp. I think I remember she said that
while laughing at us lost and unclaimed souls outside
as she barred the door from within.
I know I hate her.

Something of great value has been
snatched from me and I ache and
forget to breathe when I see
the empty shelf where I once
proudly displayed it.
Where do betrayed feelings go
when dreams are stolen?
Perhaps they are swept under faded braided
rag-rugs along with the dirt. Could be
hapless passion is sucked up by some
silent unseen cosmic vacuum cleaner alongside
life's other bothersome dust bunnies.
Maybe tattered love is carelessly discarded
beside lonely Appalachian dirt roads with
unwanted slick tires and broken rusty bedsprings
and cavalierly forgotten before the next song playing
on the car radio seeps out onto the cool, black night air.

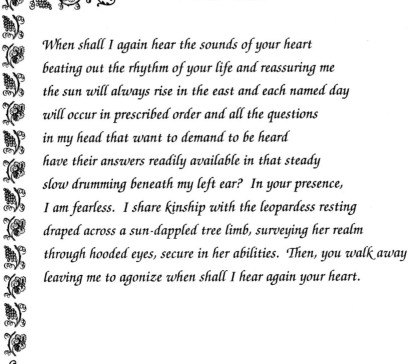

When shall I again hear the sounds of your heart
beating out the rhythm of your life and reassuring me
the sun will always rise in the east and each named day
will occur in prescribed order and all the questions
in my head that want to demand to be heard
have their answers readily available in that steady
slow drumming beneath my left ear? In your presence,
I am fearless. I share kinship with the leopardess resting
draped across a sun-dappled tree limb, surveying her realm
through hooded eyes, secure in her abilities. Then, you walk away
leaving me to agonize when shall I hear again your heart.

At that singular instant
you step out my door and disappear from sight,
niggling demons come to dance about my solitary figure,
chanting laments filled with torturing emptiness, and I
become a kitten, too soon removed from her litter,
mewing in loneliness and fright, stumbling with eyes still closed,
seeking comfort once found in the curve of another's body.
As a child, I saw my Daddy wrap raggedy toweling
about a ticking timepiece before placing it in a cardboard box
that held an orphaned tabby. His old wind-up alarm clock
was a poor substitute, but it helped that baby
make it through the night. If you can't be close,
send me a recording made of your heart's song
so I might listen to it as
I lay me down to sleep.

I require the warmth of another's body

the soothing beat of another's heart

another's arms to protect me

from howling and hungry demons

which come foraging after the sun sets.

Where are you tonight?

Don't you know how to find me?

Are you even looking?

Will I find a way to stay alive until you arrive?

The questions never change

and the answers are not forthcoming.

I know why the distant man attracts me.
I am the beggar wanting something he
doesn't have. I am the outcast never
cradled against a nurturing breast.
Ever the third thumb. Always the fifth wheel.
I've spent years and money and tears
stumbling back over forgotten childhood
paths. I accept the truth that one must love
oneself before loving another but mere
Knowledge is a dull weapon carried by
a heart that must fend for itself because when
I put my arms about me in the dark night,
it's not enough. Alone, I am not enough.

Ending

My friend is leaving
and I am the last to know.
We walked many paths together.
We laughed and suffered fools
with intolerant hearts.
My faithful companion saw me through childhood,
sat with me when I was frightened,
wept with me each time
innocence was lost
but now she is wasting away.
Medicine has no pill to cure her.
No fountain of healing waters
exists that can bring back her youth
and I am lost to know who will keep me company
until I go to be with her again.

Afraid,
you live your solitary life
keeping clear of all entanglements.

But I've had my fill of distant men:
married men seeking secreted thrills,
single men hiding behind
the skirts of work or drugs or women,
those men who sport other mistresses
while screwing me—little boys, all,
playing at being grown up.
Whichever your vice of choice,
I don't care to know.
At one time I thought I wanted
to unearth who you are.
Now I won't try to garden in your heart,
weeding out uncertainties,
tilling up hope for a future in that barren soil.

Too much
effort for such a small yield,
I'm thinking.

The Huntress

She hunted

all her life

for someone

to love her

when

all that was needed

was to love herself.

Your eyes are green gray
like the Atlantic
pelted by a driving rain
during a cold spring morning.
Maybe
the color of lichen found on a mountain boulder
along the trail to Mount LeConte would better describe them.
I seem to remember
the corners of your mouth curl up
to signal the approaching punch line.
You taste like…
Let me see…
Damn, but
I've forgotten the flavor of your kisses.
It has been far too long.
My mind's imprint of you fades and,
despite all effort to the contrary,
my heart barely feels
the poetry you wrote there.
Come back
before my body forgets as well.

"I don't miss you.

Not really,"

she explains to no one there.

"I do miss the comforting you bring

and your strength which surrounds me when you're near.

Then there is the quirkiness of your humor

and the feeling of completeness when your hand holds mine.

But I don't really miss you,"

she insists again.

No one smirks in the shadows.

"OK, maybe, just a little,"

she whispers

hoping that no one will hear.

She says to wait.
You are a man
who marks his own time.

I am intemperate.

She says to wait.
You are a man
who will not be rushed.

I have no patience.

She says to wait.
You are a man
who knows his own path.

My heart knows you
better than my head.
What she says is prudent.
I will learn
to walk alongside
your
measured
steps.
In truth,
I would not have you hurry
for I know
you will come
when you are ready.

The Visit

I traveled to you
accompanied by an entourage of expectations,
guarded by troops of past disappointments.

I reside in your land,
alongside your people,
dependent on your largess
for a while.

I wonder why I am here.
I who have fought so strenuously to depend on no man.
I who have places in my heart closed for repairs.
I who have made Solitude a blood sister.
I who have turned my back away from the one
crying out in the black hole of night
for another's heart to share.

Later, when I am safely home, I will ponder
the emotional price this visit costs,
the doors it closes,
the vistas it reveals.

Where are those counselors who advised me to consent to this journey?
What the hell was I thinking at that moment I agreed?
God is the only one who knows these answers
and even She won't share them with me.

Twenty toes uncurl. Relaxed, at last.
One mantle of cooling sweat
rests lightly over hot shoulders
as unseen disjointed body parts
spill out from invisible tattered satchels
to mingle on the rumpled sheets at our sides.

You holding me. Me holding you. Mute messages,
carried on warm breaths, breeze pass our ears.
Skin touching skin. Speechless communication
conveying libraries of thought
without the utterance of a single word.

Wondering at the wonder of it all,
heavy-lidded green eyes gaze
down into blue ones.
Both hearts confounded that
we ever found our way back,
we ancient conjoined souls
hacked apart ages past by callow youths.
While our physical bodies remain motionless,
severed ethereal organs slowly
mesh together and seamlessly meld.
Once again, we are whole.

Holding you holding me. Complete,
at last. Finally at peace within the lives
we once railed against, just wondering
at the wonder of it all.

A poetess once described
the measure of her love
to her love
by its depth and breadth.
I am too inept in the use of language for that.
I understand peace with you.
I know trust with you.
I share companionable silences with you.
Although I painstakingly cull through a tangled
jumble of verbiage to express my thoughts,
I am unwittingly betrayed
by the crudeness of my dictionary.
Intangible concepts, all grounded in you,
reside in every cell of my body.
I own them.
Ironically, I can taste your kisses. . .
trace your body's contours with my fingers. . .
even sensually act out the extent of my feelings for you,
but choosing words
to put these ideas to paper
is beyond my grasp.

Standing at the brink
I feel the dampness of the Fall's cool mist
kissing my face and bare arms,
softly brushing by my skin
like butterfly wings beating against the wind.
The emptiness in my soul is as deep as the drop
to the distant, sparkling pool
catching the water beneath me.
The ache in my heart is as ragged as the edges
on the bleak, broken rocks scattered below.

He has forsaken me for my sister.

Playing pretend, I take my first step out.
I almost feel the air rush by my ears.
I imagine the thud sound as I land.
I envision lying limp,
savoring the glorious freedom from pain.
A red-tailed hawk cries overhead.
Glancing up, I covet the ease with which she floats
the currents above me—I can do that.
Slipping off my sneakers,
I ready myself for my maiden solo flight.

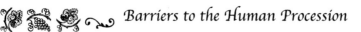

Men and women did not evolve from the same gene pool.
It is a well-documented fact.

For one,
the sexes do not possess equal internal chronometers.
"I'll call you in a few days—",
in female time, is from a few days to near seven
or thereabouts.
In male time, "in a few days"
can extend from a few days to seven years.

For some women, the time needed
for a pregnancy test to read positive
is seconds too quick;
whereas, for a man, the time
that elapses between the two-minute warning
and the last second of a televised football game
can extend up to a half hour.
And that is never long enough
for the losing team's foiled final drive.

In addition,
men and women were issued different lexicons prior to birth.
The word LOVE, in women-speak, defines a relationship
that encompasses
the sharing of two lives over time.
In man-talk,
it can mean the sharing of two bodies for a time
or until the next Right One comes along.

The two languages are as diverse
as the semantic differences between
Aussie-English and American-English
or the equivalent of a tail-wagging happy dog versus
a tail-switching mad kitty,
in that the movements are similar,
but mean quite the opposite.

It is amazing pre-humanoids ever spawned
a first generation that survived
to get on with the begats.

How come
one door must close before another can open?
How come
hearts, be they male or female, ache with the same pain?
How come
destructive relationships burn with just too much excitement,
leaving only charred, bitter regrets?
How come,
when we become adults, the lovers who kiss best
are the ones who ciphered algebra problems
one row over during high school?
How come
empowering relationships build slowly,
yet blow you away when they get
beyond the initial drag of emotional inertia?
How come
a watched phone,
like that wretched pot that never boils,
never rings?
How come
wanting to be with the object of your affection
is as strong a desire
as the craving of a crack addict for that next hit?
The Laws in physics
cannot be denied,
Axioms and Corollaries in geometry
must be proven before the student can apply them,
and The How Comes Of Love are set in stone.

Did you hear it during the night? A crack
as sharp as a rifle shot. Louder than ice
breaking up on a frozen river. During
the dark, the door guarding that treasure
she desires, so long sealed, creaked open.

Who would have ever thought that stone citadel
about his heart vulnerable? The thief inside her
who had schemed in shadows now knows,
as surely as snowdrop blossoms foretell the arrival
of spring, opportunity exists for future forays.

December Riches

Glistening stars littering a crisp, navy sky,
dissecting cold biting into exposed flesh,
snow frosting decorating the land,
hot kisses under a cool moon's icy glow
. . .gifts given as only a boy knows to give.

Twinkling lights dripping at eave's edge,
salty warmth enveloping bodies,
fronds dancing seductively to sea breeze rhythms,
hot kisses under a cool moon's icy glow
. . .gifts shared as only a man knows to share.

These Christmas memories you evoke
are not erased by the passage of time.

Days drift after days like billowing
clouds creeping across a late
afternoon sky, slower than the
molasses minutes preceding a schoolgirl's
summer vacation. Anticipation is his
drug of choice; immediate gratification,
hers. Still, she attempts mirroring his pace
but chomps on the unwelcomed control
of his strong grip, a thoroughbred
held in check, ears attuned for that sound
heralding the onset of their race.

Faded black ink traces on a tattered map scrap
kept secreted near her heart guides the way.
Crisp damp air, oozing past her face into the
warmth streaming down from the bright sky,
signals its location, luring her to the tempting inner
sanctum. She claws at its sealed closing long after
her fingers become mates to her blistered and bloodied
feet until the begrudging barrier gives way. As she
creeps inside to begin retrieval of that precious hidden
hoard, she wordlessly thanks the Powers-That-Be
for that which she had spent years seeking is now close at hand.

But the dank musty cache teasingly contains
only dustball memories of what used to be
and cobweb dreams of what never could be.

With Been-there/Done-that drumming through her brain and
echoing off stony walls in rhythm with each contraction of her
aching heart, she backs slowly away from the moldy chill
and, finally outside, crumples onto the sun-kissed ground.
Numbed by the hot glare of reality, she stares down at her
broken nails and dirty hands before crying out in disappointment,
"Is that all there is?"

"Well…yes,"
THEY—the weary parents of that headstrong child—intone.
"You always knew what the outcome would be."

What holds us back?

What ties our tongues?

What sends our frightened hearts to the ground?

Haunted pasts?

Spectral futures?

Reach out to me, my fellow prisoner of doubt.

Hand in hand, we might could finish this dance

a matched pair of silky shadows

gliding by on night's satin silence,

no longer fettered by paralyzing uncertainties.

English is a constraining framework on which
many degrees of meaning hang off a single vocalization.

I love sweet smelling gardenias, I love a groaning good pun,
I love hard-nose football, and I love your body draped over mine
speak to one muddled example.

Yet, how do I love you? Where on the sliding scale of LOVE
do you fit? By now, I would have thought someone knowledgeable
would have invented a sound, symbolized by an original collection
of characters, to identify that precious emotion
shared by two individuals.

Writers, poets and entwined couples have amassed tomes over
centuries on that tender entanglement. Recently, language
exploded to include new utterances specifically designed
for space travel and computerized communication, yet no
unique English word exists for that singular application of LOVE.

Time has come to rectify such an oversight
but where is a wordsmith wise enough to be its creator?

Just as I think it's all over,

just as I feel there's no room set aside for me in your life,

just as I steel myself to walk away,

an unexpected ring of my phone interrupts an early evening's solitude

and your honeyed voice erodes my staunch resolve,

causing me to hope once more

for shared days spent toiling by your side,

of coming nights tethered safe within your arms.

Despite my false stops, your jumpstart-calls

allow me to continue imagining us together,

let me know you hold dreams, too.

But, precious darlin', this liaison

choreographed by you

is not

for the faint of heart.

The Cake Skinner

She waits.
As she waits,
she casually nibbles,
taking care to rearrange food so
no amount appears to be missing,
but she will not help her plate
from the bounty arrayed before her.
She waits.
Having grown weary with the delay,
she stealthily skins a length of icing
from a nearby dessert with her right forefinger
and places the confection into her mouth
to verify its sweetness.
Yet she refuses to cut herself a solitary piece
because she cannot bear to eat alone.
Her party, you understand, cannot begin
without its guest of honor,
so she continues to wait
hoping he will not mind the skint cake.

I clutch illusions of us to commemorate
the comfort they once provided. They
replace the blanket I carried for security
when I was a child. I find myself afraid
to put them down, not that anyone else
covets them, by any means, but I would
feel lonely if nothing did not suddenly
appear to fill that void. I know the CPR
steps to follow lest I stumble upon an
unconscious hiker as I tramp through
the woods but please tell me the protocol for
aching hearts. Is there emergency treatment
available for near-dead hopes? And what is the
six-month prognosis should love be successfully
resuscitated? Perhaps I should simply put down these
raggedy old dreams, start sucking my thumb
and leave broken hearts to the professionals.

She's loved a man
who wasn't hers
for more years
than she cares to number
and he loves her back.
Yes, indeed, they were taught
The Rules, but along with
that first taste
of forbidden fruit
came awareness.
With each being
their Gilt Gift to the other,
both acknowledge
you must know
The Rules before
picking which ones to break.

she dines alone

she sings alone

she walks alone

she sleeps alone

she waits alone

she does object

to dancing alone

Middle-age love is endangered as any colony

of yellow lady slippers hidden in the woods;

rarer than being dealt that missing inside-straight;

for, when sitting across from a fast-fingered dealer,

we mature individuals, who are capable of intricate

intellectual feats, are instantly reduced to bumbling

novices gambling at the game of love. While staring at the

first cards spread near our drumming fingers, even as our breath

quickens with excitement, we amateurs hear that dreaded quiet chant:

The odds are with the House.

So, folding our cards,

we leave never playing out

our hand, wearing Is-That-All-There-Is masks

of scarred adults—we who were once children burned

by Desire's hot fires, whose heart rhythms

have slowed from accumulative damages,

whose lust for woodland hikes in search of

secreted blossoms has been lost. Only after languishing years perched on

hard-bottomed rockers upon Old Age's porch, do we realize, with rancor, that we have missed out on much beauty Our Mother would share

and intone with fellow weary chanters

how Youth is wasted on the foolish, foolish young

because from that jaded vantage point, we deem

early disappointments less injurious than those sustained later in life.

Having gone to those healing waters far too often, we accept blindly

the odds are always with the House.

Occasionally, however, one of us bolts out of the pack's safety

to head back into the wilds of the casino

and forgets self

and overlooks past mistakes

and ignores conventional wisdom

asking for that last card face down,

hoping to draw into a full house,

seeking that elusive perfection,

betting on a love that could possibly last

while the faint-of-heart back at the front porch mantra

"The odds are with the House."

It's not over
'til I say it's over!

But it could be over.

I know I should acknowledge
her unwanted song
and agree this game is played out.
Yet part of me hesitates,
pleading for
just a bit longer,
holding space for
that once rekindled hope.

It's time, I guess.

Funny that you heard
that siren's voice
long before me.

June 30,

Dearest Heart,

   For weeks, I've raced breakneck down deserted
country lanes, struggling to erase your imprint from my
senses, but the curve of your strong back under my fingertips
haunts my nights, the hot kiss of your whispered words
against my breast stalks my days and your memories cling as
constant as a backpack required for a month's trek across
the mountains.

   Last night while I searched in vain for sleep, I found
thoughts of you curled up beside me instead. Although more
miles than I care to count separate us, you are hardly more
than one heartbeat away.

   Do you miss me enough yet to need me with you?
Does your body wake up wondering why I don't lie close
by? How much longer do you keep me exiled?

Signed,

An inquiring heart wanting to know.

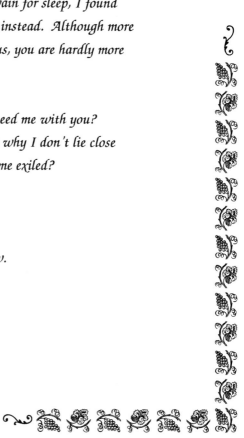

I reach for alms but my fingers remain
empty with nothing.
I search for a balm to soothe the bruisings
and find I am unable to open the jar's lid
without assistance.
I desire arms to hold me in the night,
sheltering me from that foggy
foggy dew that sneaks in soft
before dawn and condenses
in the corners of sleepless eyes.

> *Neediness is a heartless cold huntress*
> *circling easy prey and, focused on*
> *her next meal before drawing first blood*
> *on this kill, she mindlessly feeds*
> *a craving that is never satisfied.*

Wrapping about my body a tattered blanket
woven from yarns that I had spun earlier
using self-sufficient, capable fibers,
I can—I assure myself—face the long night
and the morning pearls of glistening damp.
They are, after all, merely measured segments
of my life and my own dammed tears.
Still, it would be a comfort to feel your warmth
guarding my back when I wake safe to hear
the hall clock chime two and listen
to that hungry predator's footsteps fade
as she skulks away in the darkness, thwarted.

Do I tell you
I miss you?
—existing in shadows
 without your presence to shine upon me.

Do I tell you
I think about you often?
—sending clouds
 to shower happiness on you.

Do I tell you
I talk aloud to you when you're not here?
—even waiting for your replies
 but what's bad is I sometimes hear them.

So when do I tell you
I love you?
—not till you tell me first.

One long ago Christmas
he brought her White Shoulders perfume
that he had wrapped himself in snowflake-studded tissue
paper and tied with a red satin ribbon. Being too unschooled, all
she heard was her mother's warning:

> *Beware of the offerings men give*
> *for there are always strings attached.*

At any rate, she wasn't certain he hadn't crossed over the line of
acceptable gifts for respectable girls with that bottle.

Yet, he persevered.
For formal dances, he brought her gardenia corsages when he
learned she favored those fragile blossoms whose creamy petals
were pristine and fragrant on her shoulder, bruising as easily
as the innocence of the untested heart inside her chest.

Months passed.
When she kept herself tucked inside a cocoon of unsafe naiveté, he
moved away. On an infrequent visit home, he brought her
Gibran's THE PROPHET that he had wrapped himself in heavy
brown paper and tied with white cotton twine. Alone, she then began
a quest towards enlightenment guided by the cryptic maps found
inside his token.

Years passed.

Marriages came and went. Her heart mended and broke and mended
only to break again. Once more he came back for her. They sat outside
on a wooden porch swing by a star-littered mountain stream and
listened to late night tree-frog songs and shared pieces of each other's
sagas. Still, she had more axioms to prove. So, again,
he left empty-handed.

Decades passed.

Relationships wandered in and later stumbled out of her walled
existence before she reached critical mass in her development
to emerge full grown from her confinement. One last time he came back.
With her lessons completed, she was now ready. This trip home he
brought her the tender touch of his fingertips on her cheek
and the gentle balm of his words to smooth
away the hurt-filled years. Finally she heard
the truth underlying her mother's words:

> Beware of wise men bearing gifts
>   for they will steal your heart away.

. . . telling myself you care
even though those words
never cross your lips.

. . . reminding myself you phone
as suspicion taunts
mere guilt initiates the call.

Although my lonely heart craves
to be cradled
within your strong arms,
my friends are convinced
I am only convenient
when you are here,
an inconvenience
when you are not.

You have said
you think about me every day
—little comfort
in the emptiness
of a sleepless night
when I am helplessly caught
in an endless eddy
of brackish neediness.

The myth was a comfort
as long as it lasted, but
needing more faster than
he willingly doled out, she
took too long to notice cold
hearts scorch as deep as hot stoves.
With Indifference's singular
proverb hammered home as the loser's
lonely consolation, she aches where
she was burned and knows
not to reach for him again.
Give her credit, however,
she did tell him once
she does not ask twice,
leaving him that axiom
to prove now that she is gone.

He calls

or

he doesn't call

and the sun

radiates light.

    He calls

    or

    he doesn't call

    and the moon

    wanes and waxes.

        He calls

        or

        he doesn't call

        and water droplets

        cycle between the clouds and the ground.

He calls

or

he doesn't call

and mothers pass

their mitochondria on to their offspring.

He calls

or

he doesn't call

and the food chain exchanges

proteins along its members' length.

He calls

and she senses all

is right in her world

or

he doesn't call

and she feels incapable

of finding her way through the dark;

then he calls

and her heart is able to carry on.

Children in the Woods

We each have green-slimed secrets best kept

from our civilized friends, murky memories

of personal demons fought with no regard given

to those innocents drawn into the fray. We walked

away from some conflicts bloodied but glorious victors.

When other jousts ended in unsatisfying ties, we

dragged our broken spirits across contested ground

leaving pieces of us along the way. Occasionally,

we escaped with our tails tucked between our legs,

our esteems barely intact. Our dark deeds stay behind

barriers that we erected and prefer not to cross. But for

capricious reasons, you and I agreed to reach back to

reclaim castaway cloaks of innocence left behind so long ago.

We seek refuge in the mountains where on crisp

autumn mornings we walk with unbridled joy amid shafts

of warm sunshine knifing through brown tree trunks towering

about us where slices of cloudless October-blue sky are

sandwiched between naked woody limbs knitted above. Sharing

pedestrian pleasures, we trod steep trails, hearts pounding

in unison from exertion, boots crackling through ankle-deep

gilded leaves—both rackets so deafening that we must

stop to allow sporadic spurts of conversation to be heard.

We choose to limit our intercourse these days to treks through

forests where clasped hands offer assistance over rocky

creek beds, where lips caress only a shared water bottle,

where words of heartfelt encouragement smoke out in the cool air,

where shared sensualities are not accompanied by approaching

ghosts of future yet-to-be-spoken expectations.

As old masters in the art of manipulation, we are acutely aware

of the devastation inflicted when we indulge our excesses.

Yet, by so clearly defining this couple we form, we, who have no

limits, roam free within firm boundaries and ignore the thorny taunts

coming from outside these walls, thrown by our past victims

at the children we become during our solitary duets in the woods.

The Petition

Thought he was the one
I waited for. Thought he
would light my days and
warm my nights. Thought
he would cherish me during the
quiet mist of morning, keeping
me company through this life.

Guess I was wrong.

Don't know the sign I misread.
Don't know where he geed and
I hawed. Have no idea what test
I failed. Surely, I must have
wandered into a strange classroom
and sat for the wrong exam.

Dear Mother, I've experienced all
the lessons I care to absorb. Don't wish
to learn any more, thank you!
Don't care to search for safe haven along
this dusty road again. Can my solitary
confinement be commuted to time
served? Somebody, please, beam
me up. Perhaps given another
incarnation I might get it right
and, then, I can belong somewhere
with someone the next time around.

We are sexual, not rhetorical,
in our intercourse these days.
Having dumbed down that word
to a singular physical definition,
couples share intimacies before
exchanging family histories.
Sensibility was lost years ago.
We quickly judge others inferior
without taking time to discover
their unique strengths. Blind
prejudice on our part. Believing we
can lay on hands and cure them,
we attach our hearts to crippled
personalities, never bothering to heal
ourselves. We have no sense. Shagging
the closest body at hand to while away
the time, we impatiently wait for the
appearance of that special someone
who will love and understand us. Pride
was overthrown during the revolution.
Goals have little altered since Jane Austin
put quill to paper. Marrying for love is the
carrot couples continue to chase. The parameters
of the game have changed, not the game.

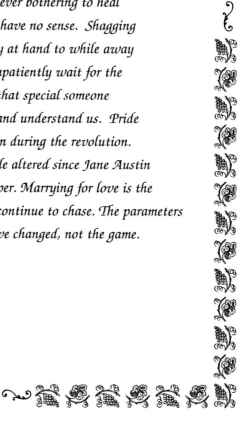

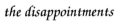

the hurts
the wounds
the disappointments
the scars that never quite silver
and fade and hair over

we all stumble
blind in a dark dank cave
because we think
loving simple
know it will cure all our ills
hope it will erase
nagging misfortunes
we are ignorant and
foolish without the light
of the enlightened
we run from commitment
fleeing chores tending love
requires...like snails
leaving silvery slime trails
through a garden of spring flowers
we harm hearts we encounter
yet are oblivious
to the beauty left marred
behind in our wakes
because our sole concern
revolves about
our gnawing emptiness

In January
you said you would
come back in March.
I wait
because I want
to believe your lies.
In any case, sweet February
is a short month.

She Wants

She wants—she's always been wanting.

She wanted as a child.

She wanted as a teenager.

She wants as a woman now.

She wants the separation to end.

She wants him, at most, a heartbeat's length away.

She wants him with her to watch the moon rise.

She wants him beside her to share dawn's soft light.

She wants it written in stone that they will never be parted.

She wants—she doesn't want much.

If you were here,
I would sit near while you worked,
writing my little lines
that don't know how to rhyme.

If you were here,
I would prepare your meals,
mend your shirts,
tend your house
because you would be husbanding me.

If you were here,
I would share my body
and partake of yours.

If you were but here,
I would sleep peacefully beside you
marking time to your breathing
with the beating of my heart.

She yearns to see his face,

to have his hands

roam her body,

to feel his breath rhythmically

against her shoulder

as they fall asleep

in the stillness

that is night.

He is not mere addiction

nor a vulgar craving.

He answers her need

for completion.

The with-whom she wants

to share mundane minutes

of middling days,

the piece missing

from her puzzle.

A phone call,

a card, a letter

offers only minimal

sustenance in the interim.

that big bed on which you sprawl will be your solitary domain,

no one will smile you a sleepy good morning as you wake,

the laundry basket will contain only your dirty clothes,

all the cats will be out of hiding,

no one will stumble behind you to the kitchen for a shared breakfast,

clean dishes will be where you can find them,

the morning paper will be read without discussion,

just one car door will be opened before you slide behind the wheel,

no one but the wind will muss your hair when you drive,

the needle will prick your finger when a button is sewn on your shirt,

the crossword puzzle will be yours to solve without assistance,

no one will snuggle close while you watch your favorite programs,

lights will remain lit until you decide it's time for them to be off,

your sheets will lose the scent of perfume,

no one will snore softly in your ear at night to interrupt your sleeping,

but you will miss me when I am gone.

She wants to be with him
but she cannot permit him
to learn the extent of her
longing. . .that's one of the
governing codes she follows.
She wants to hear his voice
but must let him call because
the gentleman is supposed to do
all the dialing. . .it's another
of the established principles
to which he adheres. They
both play out their hands,
freely allowing constraints
on their freedoms.

So,
where does it say that she
must abide by these stupid
regulations? Weren't rules
made to be broken? Who
developed these damn things
anyway? No one sane, that's
sure, and it wasn't a woman,
that's for certain. Should the
prevailing laws change,
she could choose to resume
The Game. Until then she might
as well take her board piece and
go home. Maybe there will be
another chance to play before she dies.

All her life she searched for him,

thinking she had found him

in this man here,

knowing he would be that new one

she had yet to meet there.

But he was with her all the time she was coming up,

sharing lunches in the same grammar school cafeteria,

cheering the same high school football team on nippy fall nights,

marching through the same college graduation.

He was around all that time,

waiting for her to grow up.

Heart's wings burn from exertion,

grown heavy searching for refuge.

Unable to rest nights, she glides turbulent currents in a starless sky.

The days she hunts, with hope dwindling, under a bleak white-hot sun.

Still, from her soaring heights, she can find no roost

reaching out of that murky fog-shroud roiling below.

In the past, she thought she spied branches on which to perch,

but each time drew close only to discover

her eyes had played a trick on her foolish self.

Yet she is too filled with fear to dive below those dark angry vapors

for hungry hairy monsters with sharp bloodied talons

might be lurking there to tear her to shreds.

Too proud to ask aloud for sanctuary,

she flies,

silently praying for safety

and soon, please, before

she falls

tumbling out of

the skies.

What does your housemate think of me?
This woman who once was your wife. Am
I not but a gnat to annoy her? Perhaps only
one in a long line of others. Maybe I am
nothing to her at all. I'm curious if she minds
me plundering through the pantry, treasure-hunting
through unfamiliar refrigerator shelves and
rearranging pots and pans and spices far
from their customary homes. When she returns,
will she think me blind or simply uncaring? What
will she say of my housekeeping standards when she
finds the toilet paper unrolls contrary to her preferred
installation? That will certainly let her know I was here
if she was left out of the loop! Would she be piqued if
she knew her cat sings to me while I read upon the couch?
For meals in, do I sit where she usually sits? I wonder.
Do I set the table the same as she does when she is here?
Where I must ask "What do you want for dinner?", does she
know what you want without asking? When I laugh,
do you hear her laughter? Have we lain where you once
shared her body? And perhaps, the most important query
asked last: Who is the other woman here, after all?

As your fingers caress my face,

walls guarding my heart crack.

When your lips touch mine,

all remaining defenses crumble.

After your tongue burns your mark

on my neck, I am yours for the

taking. Later your hands roam my

body and I melt into you where I

want to belong and never would

need to leave. Whisper sweet dreams

in my ear each night of my life. Hold

me close as I slip away to sleep. Never

allow me to greet daybreak without

your warmth beside mine. After you grant

these little wishes, I will own the most

envied heart in the world.

By myself I have fashioned a life,
purchased a house, feathered a nest.
If you were here, we could create a home.
I sing songs that never reach your ears.

    Will you ever hear them?

I walk mountain trails alone.

    Will you be here soon?

I hug myself close at night wishing
my arms were your arms holding me.

    Why aren't they?

My cat sleeps nestled
in the crook of my knee.

    Are you here yet?

My heart needs to believe the fairy tales
about princes that come someday. I only
hope that you arrive before I grow too old
to want to ask,

    Where are you tonight?

    I can't feel you breathing.

What if she goes
and she becomes bored with him
during the drive from the airport?

What if she goes
and he grows weary of her
after the first night?

What if she goes
and she doesn't want
to return home?

What if she goes
and he is not the man
she pretended him to be?

What if she goes
and they find they possess
each other's missing pieces?

What if she goes
and she exposes her vulnerability
only to find he gigs her?

What if she goes
and he doesn't want
her to leave?

What if she goes
and she is completely
out of her element?

What if she goes
and he chooses
to make no place for her?

What if she goes
and they can unearth
no common ground?

What if she doesn't go?
Then, she will never know.

…quiet hours spent under gray skies
wondering why you keep me at arm's length.

Your life is richly sweet without me.
So, why am I here? I keep asking.
We must be too many questions
you do not care to confront at this time.
Just how will you justify me to all those inhabiting your world?
Can you still meet their selfish expectations
and show up with me at your side?

It's easier to take me around strangers
where we appear to be the couple they assume us to be.
So, when I happen to touch your arm,
you won't need to panic lest
familiar eyes observe my show of affection.
And if I should gaze upon your face,
you'll have no need to shield your emotions from
those who read the sentiments displayed.

You must have realized early on
that I am a poor actress.
I am much too old to play pretend.
Maybe that is why you won't let me near you.
You have discovered too late
that I am too much icing for your cake.

Name the rule I bent.

    Did I smile too brightly when you gathered me at the airport?

    Did our skins feel too vibrant after that first touching?

    Did you feel too comfortable as we walked and held hands?

Name the infraction I committed.

    Did I taste too sweet when you kissed me?

    Did we mesh too easily into a smooth routine?

    Did you relax too deeply against my body in the darkness?

Name the misdemeanor for which I stand accused.

    Did I get too close for your comfort?

    Did our bodies move too good together?

    Did you sweat too much after you had me?

Well, then, go ahead, judge me guilty
on all counts before sentencing me back
to the mountains from whence I came.
I am only here because you asked me.
Truth is, I would gladly travel back
should you invite me again.

By the way, there is one offense I demand to plea bargain.

    If it's about your gardenias,

    I couldn't help but bruise a few petals.

DUMB
adj., destitute of the power of speech

Over the years I have thought of you plenty.
Sometimes I see the future and have known
one day you would come back. Twice
I have been told by mystics to expect you.

Yet I am awed that you and I are here
together at all for we are but shy foolish
children rich with fistfuls of do-over cards
who still can't play well with each other.

Could be we are O. Henry-penned lovers incarnate,
scripted never to be on the same page for it seems
I'm always cutting my hair and you're always
selling your watch no matter the decade
in which we reside. Maybe we are proverbial
cruelly-tested Greek lovers fated never to touch,
destined to wander alone through wastelands
populated by hordes looking for that one promised hand.

At present we sit at desks yards apart
in the same room and I wonder how
we will fashion a life together when
we can't even catch the same wave.
We must be the definition of dumb
personified. All that we could be together
will never be allowed to be because I sit
in silence scribbling on paper while you sit
quietly tapping computer keys.

The tangle of it all, that rat's nest

which prevents me spinning free,

is that little ol' issue of trust.

ISSUE is such a pasteurized, passionless,

tame word to describe the cold, filthy, feral

terror circling about my suspicioning heart.

TRUST... what's that? After years of betrayals,

after lies upon lies, after slashes that sliced deep

into unprotected innocence. Just how does one trust?

After decades of misjudging character,

after disappointments numbering more

than the spots on a set of ivory dominoes,

after blindly stumbling into sharp-cornered emotions

in pitch-dark hearts. Trust whom? First, I must trust

me to trust you. A laughable predicament, wouldn't

you agree? A storyline divined to put O. Henry

in hog heaven, I'm thinking.

Have you ever been
as lonely as me?
Have you ever hiked
empty trails through forests
filled with friends and felt alone?
She has questions,
but what she voices is a safe
How was your day?

Miles separate them.
Telephones link them.
Words ill define
their true conversation
where sounds brush by ears
like soft kisses and pauses caress
as gently as tentative fingertips.
Nickels stack up.
Minutes slide by.
Finally with reluctance, she says,
Well, guess you'd better let me go.

What do you have planned for tomorrow?
is his generic response while
what he wants to ask is:
Have you ever strolled
down a crowded beach
and yours are the only footsteps in the sand?
Have you ever been
as lonely as me?

Do you hear my song?

Can you hum the tune?

Do you know the words?

If I sing softly,

will you hear me?

If I shout the lyrics,

will you cover your ears

and turn away?

If we sing together,

will we keep

the same tempo?

If I lose my place,

will you show me

where we are?

Do I hear your song?

Can I sing harmony

to your melody?

Do I, perhaps, simply hear

separate solos?

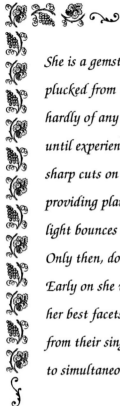

She is a gemstone

plucked from the muck,

hardly of any interest

until experience creates

sharp cuts on her exterior,

providing planes on which

light bounces against and plays upon.

Only then, does she glimmer and sparkle.

Early on she was schooled how to present

her best facets to others but, mercifully,

from their singular vantage points, they are unable

to simultaneously view every slice she has endured.

She is a long corridor

lined with closed doors.

As spectators stroll her length,

certain doors open to allow

glimpses into the rooms of her past.

Some doors swing full wide on oiled hinges.

Others barely creak open an inch.

Still more, held fast by rusty locks,

don't move at all, not even for her,

for long ago she hid their keys for safekeeping.

She is a woman-child,

with sloe eyes hooded,

undulating around flickering flame tongues

centered upon ancient desert sands.

Draped in gossamer lengths of rainbow hues, she

tempts her master's eyes with artful flashes of soft skin,

spinning to expose a line of long thigh or the curve of a full breast,

seductively dropping one piece of transparent silk

onto the sand, possibly, even two. Yet she clutches

tightly to the remaining five veils

obscuring full view of her swaying body.

We women are actors, all,

hidden behind grease paint smears

stiffly posturing upon life's stage

too afraid to bare our fragile selves.

In dimmed light,

we stand as close as pages in a closed book

my breathing conforming to yours,

my forehead nestles into the curve

where your angel-wings would attach.

    If you had any.

Your graying head lowers,

your weight shifts, settling squarely over your feet.

My arms reach under your arms

to clasp you against my breasts.

Filled with unspoken doubts,

we gingerly lean into each other

seeking support. My palms roam

the rugged contours of your naked chest

like fingers of the blind searching

passages. My tongue traces soft webs

of wet kisses onto your salty muscular back.

All the while, you remain as patient

as a seasoned war-horse caught

in an open field, waiting out a summer shower,

your head bowed as sensations rain against you.

In our youth, you had kissed me

until my mouth was bruised and bloodied.

In that long ago darkness, your coltish body

had felt too unschooled, too untempered,

too smooth. Tonight you return as a man,

at ease within your masculinity, your chest

now measuring greater than mine. Your

powerful body is cloaked in downy, wiry

male hair; your protection is there for my asking.

> *Should I need it.*

In our spring, we had hurried and fumbled

too green to wait for the waiting to become

unbearable. In our autumn, we linger and caress

and understand to wait for the waiting to become

almost past pleasurable. Our old hearts are weary,

wary veterans of the love wars people are wont

to stage. They are gnarled and crisscrossed with scars

received during many a skirmish. And mine wants to hope

that this time the outcome could be different.

 The Dinner Guest

He phoned. Said he wanted to see her.
The reason why she doesn't know
and didn't think to ask. Neither did
she question the vagaries of life's currents.
After all, they had known each other far too long,
exchanged season's greetings for too many Decembers.

To dinner she heard herself invite him
but it was too soon after the betrayal
for her to be alone with a man.
Just the two of them. A man there
within her walls, alone with her.

To put unease at ease,
she hastily recruited others. During
the first glass of wine, the six chorused
they liked him better than the Betrayer
whom no one had liked but her. Accepting
each backdoor compliment with grace
alongside the cheese and crackers, he meshed
with the guardian friends. Later he stayed
after the goodnights were said
to clear away the plates.

He did more that evening than the dishes.
Surrounded by his strong arms, her heart
came to settle in its home within her house
under spring's full moon.

Maybe if
he lifted the bar and
pushed open that massive door,
she could gain access to the fortress
he so artfully erected about himself.
Maybe if
he relaxed his stance, she could
curl her body into his and
they could create a sum
greater than their two parts.
Maybe before
she becomes frustrated in her attempts
to teach a reluctant swine with
four left feet the waltz...
Maybe before
her heart exhausts all hope...
Maybe when
rocks gain a social conscience...
Maybe when
hippos fly....

David Sleeps

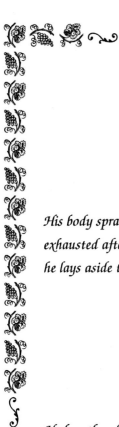

After the last gawkers have meandered out
and all museum doors are secured, Michelangelo's
David steps down from his pedestal. Shaking
off the droppings left by admiring eyes, Perfection
unburdens himself for the coming of night.

His body sprawls across the couch where he has fallen
exhausted after the day's battles. While the world news airs,
he lays aside the cares of work and I clear away supper.

What is that nameless something that makes a man
appear utterly defenseless while he sleeps, changing
any woman stumbling upon him into Athena
who, without hesitation, guards him while he is down?

He breathes deep and gives in when I ease beside him
in the early evening stillness. While he floats on
that dense heavy mist between awareness and asleep,
he pulls me close to him and we become one,
sharing the wealth of our warmth. But she lurks
in the shadows nearby, cackling low through thin
parched lips, and I wish I had no ears to hear
Tragedy's mirthless laugh, for my beloved makes
no room for me while he is awake.

I could have entrusted my life
to the one who was a master at survival arts,
which is a most desirable trait
should civilization as we know it end.

I could have entrusted my future
to the man who was an industrial captain,
commanding hordes of stocks and bonds,
and look forward to a financially secure old age.

I could have entrusted my being
to him who knew his way around
a woman's body as well as any man-child
knows the woods behind his house,
but that would have gotten old since
he didn't have any other hobbies.

They just could never do,
and I am glad that I waited
because I can trust my heart to you.

Cruel Time

minutes crawl by

time is uncaring

you'll be in my arms soon

I'll deal

with those heartless clocks

later

I scratch black marks on white paper.

In truth, the quill is dipped in my heart's blood.

I show the scribbles to strangers

and, with faked dispassion, search their faces for approval,

frightened to show my feelings to the one who matters.

Afraid a man would understand

and know me and stay.

Afraid a boy would misunderstand

and laugh and run away to play.

Love is fire.

It can make you sweat.

Running out of control,

it chars everything in its path.

Confined to a safe size,

it is a pleasurable comfort.

Tend it too close

and you might knock it down.

Feed it too fast

and you smother it.

Add no fuel

and you watch it die

from lack of attention.

Poking around with both

is mesmerizing to most

and a favorite pastime for some.

And when either is gone,

you fear the cold.

We are a campaigning politician

when we promise our lovers,

I am simply who I am,

courting their hearts with

only the agendas we

deem necessary to reveal.

Simplicity in being

does not exist.

Full disclosure is

never needed. Some doors

should remain unopened.

Some events do not

need to be revisited.

Lovers, at best,

proffer half-truths.

That's the reality.

Really.

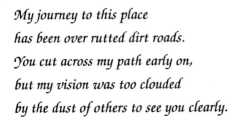

My journey to this place
has been over rutted dirt roads.
You cut across my path early on,
but my vision was too clouded
by the dust of others to see you clearly.

My trek to here has been
what it has been. Along the way,
I have been set upon by bandits
who were once perceived as friends.
Despite those betrayals or perhaps
because of those betrayers,
I yearn for the protection
your arms might could offer
as we travel on.

Are you friend or are you adversary?
Will you guard my back as I watch
yours or do we shake hands after
the sun's rising to bid each other
safe journey before heading out on
our separate ways?

searching one final time

through the rubble of discarded tattered dreams

gnarled fingers happen upon an earthen clump

> Could this conceal the rare treasure so long sought?

> Might the nay-sayers possibly be wrong?

clutching the encrusted find against her pounding breast

jealously guarding it from all prying eyes

secretly she cries

in hope

in fear

in love

in vain

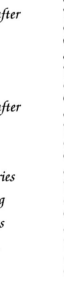

Long after
music
drifts
away
Long after
ink
fades
Memories
evoking
caresses
remain

Other Books by Nancy Melinda Hunley:

What if you meet a stranger during a hike and he turns out to be your long, lost love? This is the premise for Hunley's first novel, *This Time Around*, released April, 2004.

". . .a comic southern tale. . .a great read for East Tennesseans. Heck, we're all in there." *Halls Shopper News*, February 23, 2004

". . .romance infused with local flavor. . ." *Knoxville News Sentinel*, March 14, 2004

❧

Southern Graces, an Incompleat Manual for Feminine Deportment, is a satirical look back at the instructions that East Tennessee mothers doled out before the E.R.A. era. Due for release before January, 2005.

❧

The following is the introduction to *The Edisto Games*, Hunley's second novel which is currently under construction:

"Upon reviewing a map, you can see that the Edisto River links the interior of South Carolina with the Atlantic. The river meanders roughly ninety miles from near Aiken on down to just above Beaufort on the coast. While standing on its banks, you can peer no more than a few inches into its murky depths. That fact alone marks the river as unique because the world has only a handful of black water rivers.

"Where the Edisto runs through the public rose gardens in the thriving community of Snowshill, its waters are cold and fast and dark. Just like the heart of Hamp Sellers."

Nancy Melinda Hunley is a retired dentist living in Knoxville, Tennessee. A third book entitled, *Southern Graces*, will be available shortly. She is currently at work on a second novel, *The Edisto Games*.

For updates, go to www.nmhunley.com

Printed in the United States
22040LVS00005B/532-567

9 780974 283012